STEM Projects in **MINECRAFT**™

The Unofficial Guide to

Building Skyscrapers in

MINECRAFT™

RYAN NAGELHOUT

PowerKiDS
press.

New York

Published in 2019 by The Rosen Publishing Group, Inc.
29 East 21st Street, New York, NY 10010

First Edition

Editor: Greg Roza
Book Design: Rachel Rising
Illustrator: Matías Lapegüe

Photo Credits: Cover, pp. 1, 3, 4, 6, 8, 10, 12, 14, 16, 18, 20, 22, 23, 24 Evgeniy Dzyuba/Shutterstock.com; p. 4 Zoltan Gabor/Shutterstock.com; pp. 6, 8, 12, 14, 16, 18 Levent Konuk/Shutterstock.com; p. 7 Kokliang/Shutterstock.com; p. 8 NAAN/Shutterstock.com; p. 19 Songquan Deng/Shutterstock.com; p. 20 Irina Kosareva/Shutterstock.com; p. 22 carballo/Shutterstock.com.

Library of Congress Cataloging-in-Publication Data

Names: Nagelhout, Ryan, author.
Title: The unofficial guide to building skyscrapers in Minecraft / Ryan Nagelhout.
Description: New York : PowerKids Press, 2019. | Series: STEM projects in Minecraft | Includes index.
Identifiers: LCCN 2017057840| ISBN 9781508169376 (library bound) | ISBN 9781538329450 (pbk.) | ISBN 9781538329467 (6 pack)
Subjects: LCSH: Minecraft (Game)–Handbooks, manuals, etc.–Juvenile literature. | Skyscrapers–Design and construction–Juvenile literature.
Classification: LCC GV1469.M55 N34 2019 | DDC 794.8–dc23
LC record available at https://lccn.loc.gov/2017057840

Manufactured in the United States of America

CPSIA Compliance Information: Batch #CS18PK: For Further Information contact Rosen Publishing, New York, New York at 1-800-237-9932

Contents

The World Above

Minecraft is a game where you can dig deep under the ground. Valuable **resources** are buried there, and the player can go get these items by exploring tunnels and using tools to mine them. The resources can then be used to make all kinds of different things, such as more tools and weapons.

However, the space above the ground is yours to craft, too! Building a place to put your things and stay safe at night is important. Bigger projects, such as skyscrapers, can be even more fun. And a bunch of different skyscrapers together can be used to make a city!

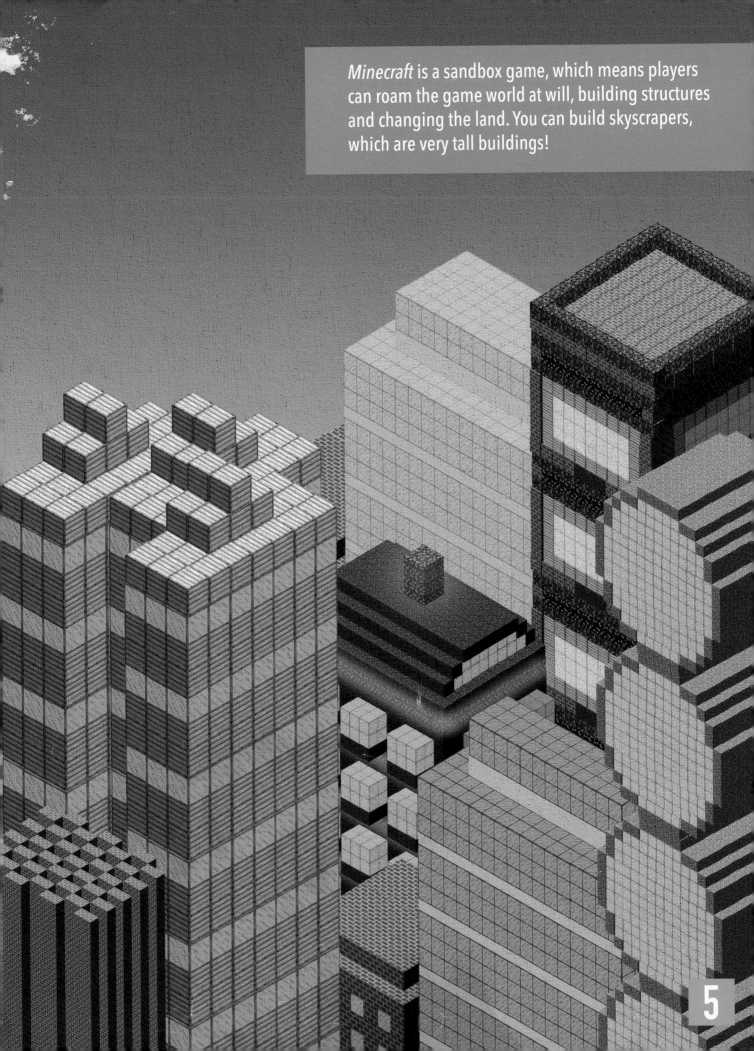

Minecraft is a sandbox game, which means players can roam the game world at will, building structures and changing the land. You can build skyscrapers, which are very tall buildings!

Building Up Resources

Minecraft is a game where you can do pretty much anything you want. However, the game **mode** in which you play affects how hard it is to build things. In Survival mode, players must find, mine, or craft everything they use in the game. They also must eat and avoid getting sick! Finding enough resources to build what you want might take a long time.

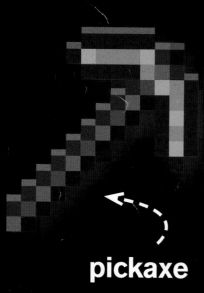

pickaxe

In Creative mode, however, you get every single block in the game to use right away. You can also fly! This will help you build things faster without the use of **scaffolding** or stairs.

MINECRAFT MANIA

Even making the right tools to mine things may take time. Mining rare resources such as gold or diamonds requires at least a pickaxe made of iron. If you use a stone pickaxe, the block will just break!

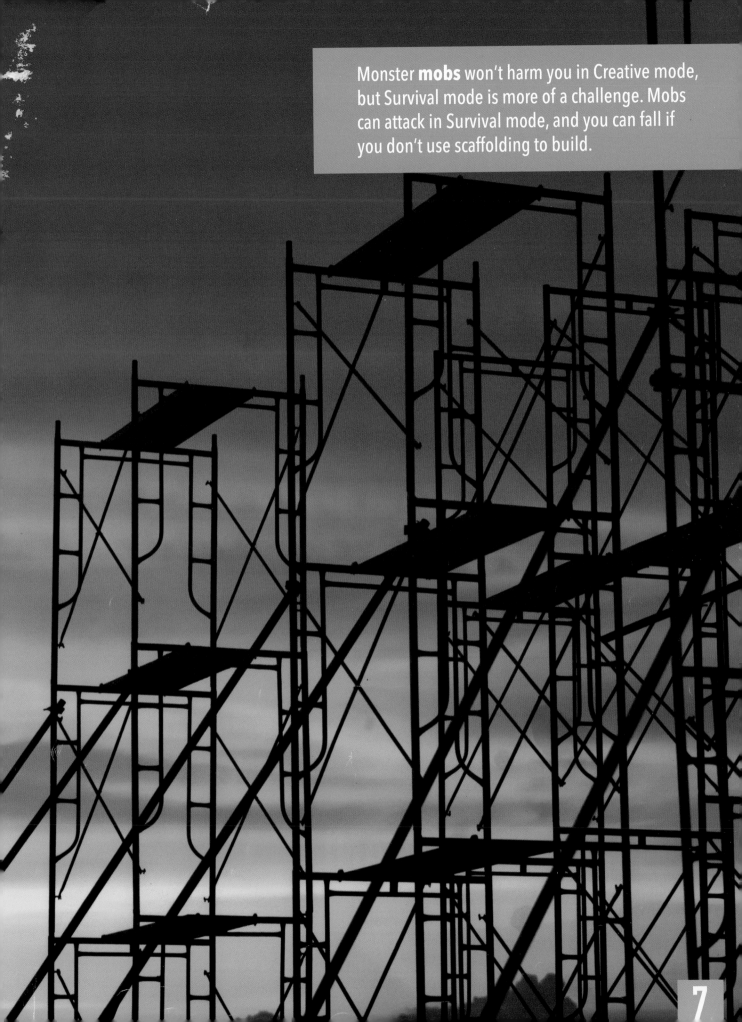

Monster **mobs** won't harm you in Creative mode, but Survival mode is more of a challenge. Mobs can attack in Survival mode, and you can fall if you don't use scaffolding to build.

Use the Right Blocks

When you're building a skyscraper, the first thing you must decide is what kind of blocks you'll use. You can make skyscrapers out of many kinds of blocks, but you must make sure you have enough of whatever kind you use.

Most modern skyscrapers in the real world are made of metal and glass. But iron blocks are a challenge to get in Survival mode. You must mine iron ore deep underground. It takes nine pieces of ore to make just one iron block. It's often easier to make skyscrapers out of stone resources rather than metal in *Minecraft!*

MINECRAFT MANIA

Blocks of glowstone look cool and give off light. However, you must travel to the Nether–a very dangerous, fiery place–to find them in Survival mode.

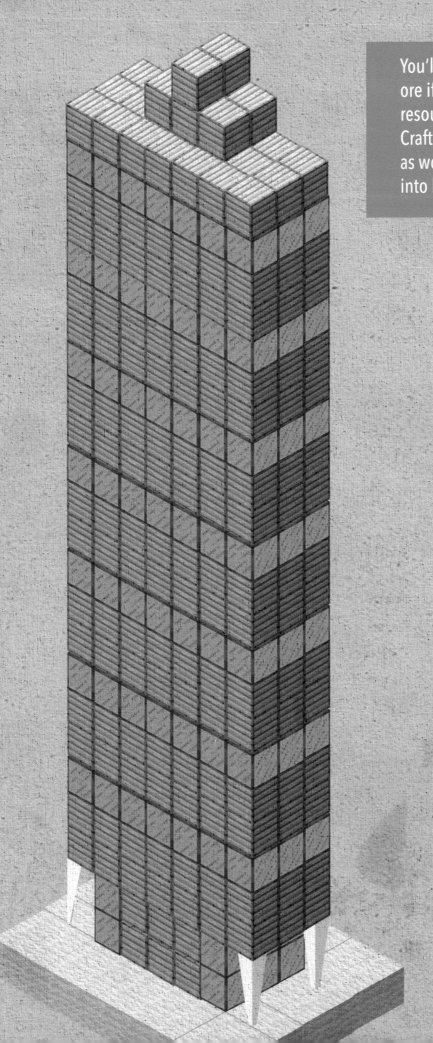

You'll need to **smelt** some ore if you want to make metal resources to build skyscrapers. Craft a furnace and use fuel such as wood or coal to turn the ore into bars called ingots.

Cobble and Sand

In Creative mode, it's easy to build with metal and glass, but building a skyscraper in Survival mode is hard! You might want to build a skyscraper out of resources you can get easily. For example, you can get lots of cobblestone (a type of stone block with many cracks in it) from mining basic gray stone. These rocks only drop cobblestone when mined.

However, if you add cobblestone to a furnace with fuel in it, the cobblestone will turn back into regular stone. You can also look in sandy areas to find lots of sandstone, or you can craft lots of sand into sandstone!

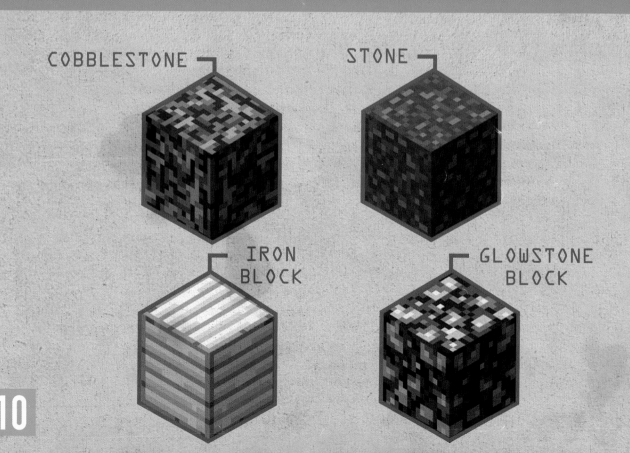

COBBLESTONE

STONE

IRON
BLOCK

GLOWSTONE
BLOCK

A crafting table can help you make different kinds of resources into other things. Make sure you check what resources you have and what they can be turned into.

Design and Form

In the real world, people make skyscrapers using **designs** that let the buildings rise very high in the air. Many of the different parts of a skyscraper's design make it safer to build the structure taller. A big, tall building needs a strong foundation, or base, to hold its weight. This spreads the downward pull of gravity on the building over a wider area.

In *Minecraft,* though, most blocks aren't affected by gravity, which means you can stack them high without worrying about them falling. In fact, the only thing that stops your skyscraper from going higher is the size of the **chunk** in the game: it's 256 blocks high.

MINECRAFT MANIA

Gravity affects blocks such as sand and gravel. If there isn't another block resting underneath these blocks, they'll fall!

One great thing about a skyscraper in *Minecraft* is that it's very tall, so it's easy to see from far away. You can even see the building at night if you light it up using torches or glowstone.

Form or Function?

If you want to make a skyscraper you can use as a home or base, you'll need to build it so people can go inside. That means making a door and floors inside it. You have to decide how tall each floor of the skyscraper will be. Each floor needs to be at least two blocks tall for your character to walk inside.

If you're just building a skyscraper for show, though, you don't need to worry about the inside. It can be empty in there, and you can build it as tall as you want without worrying about how many floors it is.

MINECRAFT MANIA

Most floors of a skyscraper are the same height, but sometimes the top or bottom floors can be bigger. Some skyscrapers have huge open **lobbies** that take up the space of many floors.

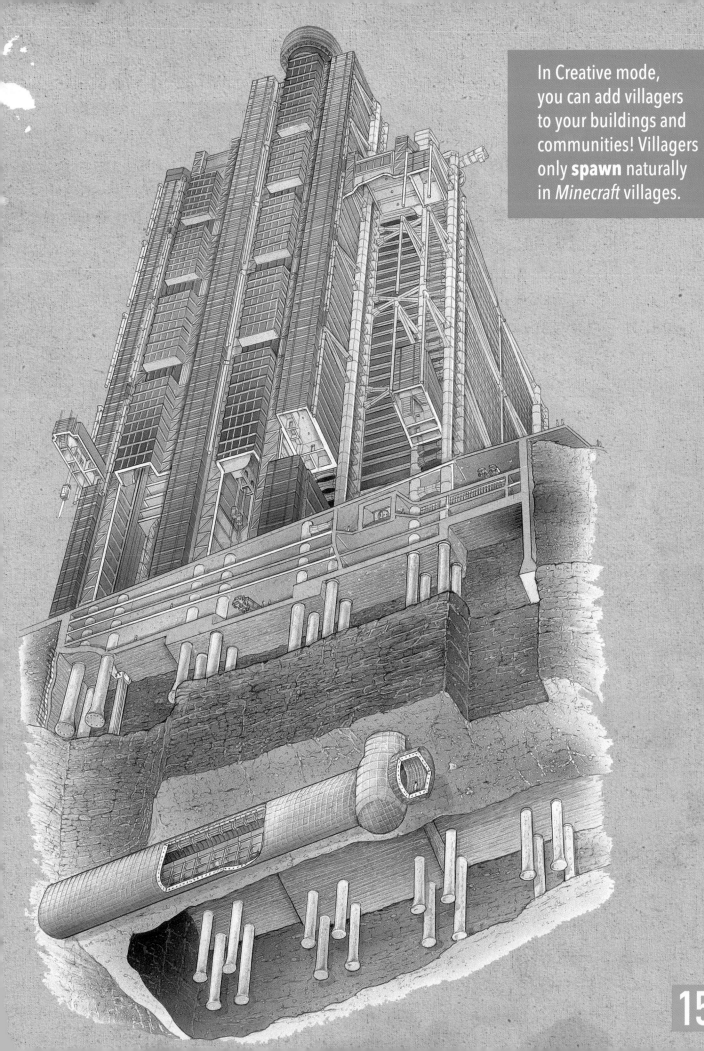

In Creative mode, you can add villagers to your buildings and communities! Villagers only **spawn** naturally in *Minecraft* villages.

Base and Footprint

Planning is important when you're building skyscrapers. Think about how big the base of your skyscraper should be. This is called its footprint. It might be easier to dig down in the dirt and put a base layer of rock down so you know how big your footprint will be.

In the real world, many skyscrapers' footprints are squares or rectangles. Some are circles. But you can build a skyscraper in *Minecraft* in any shape. It can even look like a creeper! You could put a water block at the top and add a waterfall to your skyscraper.

MINECRAFT MANIA

Skyscrapers are more eye catching if you use different colors and kinds of blocks. You can make a pattern and use it throughout your skyscraper, inside and out!

Water blocks can be scooped up with a bucket. You can add interesting water features such as waterfalls to your skyscraper.

Kinds of Skyscrapers

You can build any skyscraper you want in *Minecraft*, but it may not look like a real one unless you follow some rules used to make skyscrapers in real life. One of the earlier skyscraper styles is called Chicago, or **Commercial**, style. These buildings usually have a strong foundation, a metal frame, at least five floors, and many windows.

You can design skyscrapers that have huge top floors with great views of your *Minecraft* world. You can also make big buildings out of stone or concrete with only a few small windows. This is like a style called brutalism!

MINECRAFT MANIA

In *Minecraft*, you can use redstone to make blocks move. It's sort of like electricity in *Minecraft*! You can even make elevators for your skyscrapers with redstone.

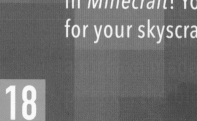

Sometimes skyscrapers reflect the things in nature around them. Can you build a skyscraper that looks like a mountain?

19

Make It Yours

Many modern skyscrapers use lots of glass. Some also have tall points on top that make them even taller. These are called spires. A spire can make your building visible from even farther away! Many famous skyscrapers have spires, including the Empire State Building in New York City.

With no gravity to battle, you can make your skyscraper into all kinds of shapes. You can build bridges, or **spans**, between your skyscrapers to connect them. And you can make colored, or stained, glass by adding dyes to glass blocks or panes after you craft them! *Minecraft* has many colorful blocks.

Empire State Building

In *Minecraft*, the only limit on what you can build is what you can imagine. Look at different skyscraper designs and try making your own!

Making Mods

You can make your *Minecraft* creations even more exciting with modifications, or mods. Using a computer program called ScriptCraft, you can create new blocks, change the way the game functions, and make your own games. Imagine what you could build! You could build a skyscraper out of gingerbread or candy, like something from a modern fairy tale. Or you could build a skyscraper that changes colors or glows in the dark!

If you're interested in learning how to create mods in *Minecraft*, visit the website below. You'll find the information needed to get started with ScriptCraft and build your own *Minecraft* mods.

https://scriptcraftjs.org

Glossary

chunk: A segment, or part, in the Minecraft world. One chunk is 16 blocks wide, 16 blocks long, and 256 blocks high.

commercial: Having to do with commerce, or the large-scale buying and selling of goods and services.

design: The pattern or shape of something. Also, to create the pattern or shape of something.

lobby: A hall or entry room large enough to hold people who are waiting.

mob: A moving creature within *Minecraft*. Often used to mean one of the monsters that spawns in *Minecraft* at night.

mode: A form of something that is different from other forms of the same thing.

resource: Something that can be used.

scaffolding: A system of scaffolds, or raised platforms for workers to sit or stand on.

smelt: To heat to separate metals.

span: The flat part of a bridge that stretches over a length and is supported by the rest of the bridge.

spawn: To bring forth. In video games, when characters suddenly appear in a certain place.

Index

C
coal, 9
concrete, 18
Creative mode,
      6, 7, 10, 15

D
diamonds, 6

E
elevator, 18

F
foundation, 12, 18

G
glass, 8, 10, 20
glowstone, 8,
     10, 13
gold, 6
gravel, 12
gravity, 12, 20

I
iron, 6, 8, 10

M
mobs, 7
modifications
     (mods), 22

N
Nether, 8

O
ore, 8, 9

P
pickaxe, 6

R
redstone, 18

S
sand, 10, 12
ScriptCraft, 22
spans, 20
spires, 20
stone, 6, 8, 10
Survival mode, 6,
     7, 8, 10

V
villagers, 15

W
water, 16
wood, 9

Websites

Due to the changing nature of Internet links, PowerKids Press has developed an online list of websites related to the subject of this book. This site is updated regularly. Please use this link to access the list:
www.powerkidslinks.com/stemmc/skyscrapers